Published in 2013 by Wayland
Text copyright © Pat Thomas 2013
Illustrations copyright © Lesley Harker 2013

Wayland
Hachette Children's Books
338, Euston Road,
London NW1 3BH

Wayland Australia
Level 17/207 Kent Street
Sydney, NSW 2000

Concept design: Kate Buxton
Series design: Paul Cherrill for Basement68
Editor: Victoria Brooker

British Library Cataloguing in Publication Data
Thomas, Pat, 1959-
A parent in the armed forces. -- (A first look at)
1. Families of military personnel--Pictorial works--
Juvenile literature. 2. Soldiers--Family relationships--
Pictorial works--Juvenile literature. 3. Separation
(Psychology)--Pictorial works--Juvenile literature.
I. Title II. Series III. Harker, Lesley.
155.4'4-dc23

ISBN: 978 0 7502 7855 3

2 4 6 8 10 9 7 5 3 1

Printed in China

Wayland is a division of Hachette Children's Books,
an Hachette UK company.
www.hachette.co.uk

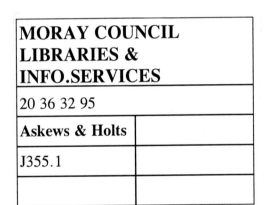

Come Home Soon

A FIRST LOOK AT A PARENT IN THE ARMED FORCES

PAT THOMAS
ILLUSTRATED BY LESLEY HARKER

WAYLAND

Saying goodbye to someone you love is never easy.

But when your family has someone
in the military, saying goodbye is
something everyone has to learn about.

If you have a parent in the military then
their job is to help keep the peace –
and sometimes to fight a war.

Although most parents do their jobs at home or near where they live, military parents sometimes have to travel far away from home to do theirs.

When you know that your parent is going away it's normal to feel lots of things all at once.

You may feel cross that they are leaving, and scared they might not come back.

You may feel worried that your parent may forget about you while they are away...

...but that will never happen.

What about you?

Do you know other children who have parents in the military? What do you know about your parent's job? What are some of the things you feel about them going away?

You'll have lots of questions too, like:

Where are you going?

Why are you going?

What are you going to do there?

When will you be back?

Go ahead and ask. Chances are
everyone in your family is wondering
the same things and asking questions will
give you all a chance to talk it through.

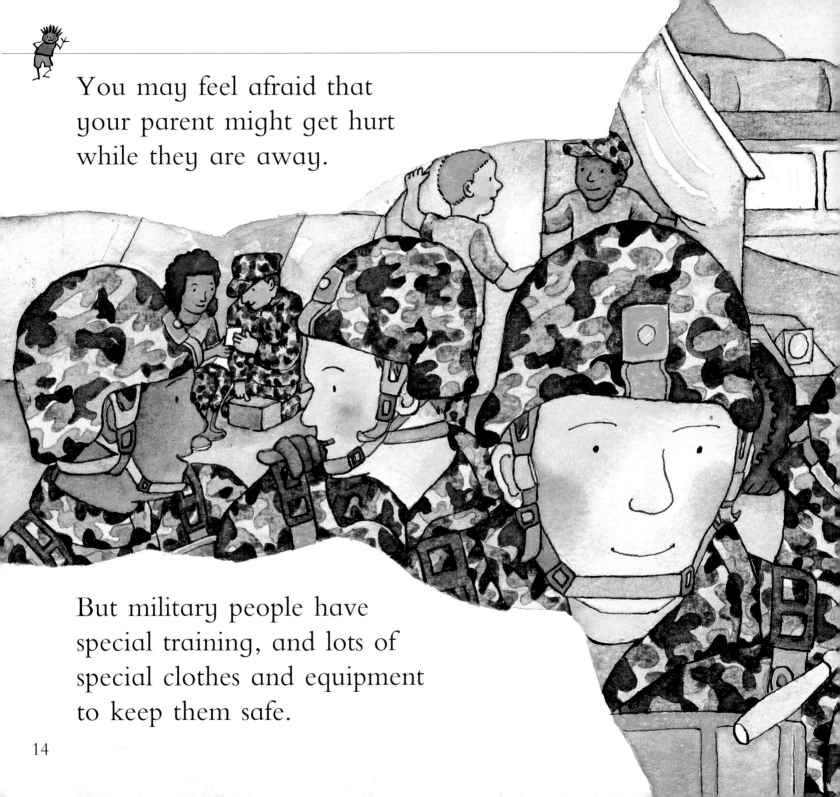

You may feel afraid that your parent might get hurt while they are away.

But military people have special training, and lots of special clothes and equipment to keep them safe.

14

They also have lots of other men and women around them who know how important it is to look after each other so they can all get home safely to their families.

When a parent goes
away, some things
can change at home.
Everyone can feel
a bit upset
and confused.

And with
one less person at
home there may be more
chores for everyone to do.

That can be a pain. But it also gives everyone
a chance to learn to do new things and help
each other in new ways.

What about you?

How do you help around the house at the moment? What
things might change at home with a parent away? What do
you miss most about not having your parent there?

While your parent is away you can still keep in touch by sending emails and packages with special treats.

You can talk on the phone sometimes too.

You can also feel closer to them by keeping pictures of them where you can always see them...

...and keeping a special calendar that shows how soon they will be home.

It may seem like your parent is very far away. But wherever we are everyone on earth shares the same sky.

When you are missing your parent look up and know that they can see the same sun, and the same moon and stars that you can.

What about you?

What are some of the things you and your family can do to feel closer to your parent while they're away?

Remember also that you are
loved and missed and that
there is a special place
in your parent's heart
just for you.

22

Your parent is doing a job that he or she feels is very important and as soon as it's done you can all be together again.

While your parent has been away everyone in the family will have grown and seen and learned new things.

It can take a while to get to know each other again.

Lots of love and patience will help things
get back to normal for everyone.

Saying goodbye can be sad...

26

But saying hello again can be
one of the happiest times that
you all share as a family.

HOW TO USE THIS BOOK

When a parent is deployed to war it can be very disruptive to the whole family. Young children, however, may have less resources available to them to express or make sense of how they feel. This book is meant to be read with your child, more than once, and used as both a comfort and a starting place for discussion. Try reading it through first and familiarising yourself with its content before you begin.

The best way for you to help your child cope is to be sure you feel ready to cope. Your child draws strength and confidence from you so make sure you and your partner are prepared both practically and emotionally and are clear in your plans. Give your child as much notice as possible pre-deployment and, if you are able to, try to draw the adult support you need from friends and family and social groups during deployment and beyond.

With so much to do pre-deployment it can be difficult, but try to spend as much time as possible just being with your child before you go.

For young children the concept of a long separation can be hard to grasp. Keeping a visual reminder such as a calendar where your child can check the dates off can be helpful.

Your child may be concerned about the disruption of his or her normal routine and have questions about who will take them to school, whether their parent will be home in time for their birthday or a holiday. A young child may ask such questions over and over again. Be patient and reassuring as it can take children a long time to fully absorb the information.

Before deployment you may also want to create a memento for your child (or individual ones for each child, including teenagers). Record yourself reading books, create a personal photo album of time together. Arrange pictures of you around the house (don't be camera shy - remember you're doing this for them). If you are going to be gone a long time, write up cards or buy presents 'from you' for anticipated special occasions you'll miss.

Find ways to stay connected. Exchange keepsakes and photos, send emails and letters, arrange for regular phone calls if this is possible — it all helps reinforce a sense of connection. At the same time reassure your child that there may be times you can't be in touch, but that doesn't mean anything is wrong or that you have forgotten about them.

While one parent is away try to stick to family routines and traditions. Keep schedules for mealtimes and bedtimes, go on vacations and celebrate the holidays and special occasions as you would if the absent parent was there.

A parent returning home from war can sometimes have a difficult time adjusting to civilian life. Help your child understand that everyone will need to be patient as routines get back to normal.

Keep teachers in the loop. The stability and normal routines of school are an important anchor for children during deployment. Teachers can be on the lookout for signs your child is not coping well.

Teachers, parents and students may benefit from thoughtful discussions about the military and war and the effects it is having on them. It is important to be sensitive to the fact that some children with direct experience of this will be more affected by such discussions. Classroom discussions, perhaps with an invited guest from the military, can be a safe environment where children can ask questions and build an understanding of military life, but also how they can be helpful and supportive to friends and family members directly impacted by such things.

BOOKS TO READ

For children
Lily Hates Goodbyes
Jerily Marler and Nathan Stoltenberg
(Wyatt-MacKenzie Publishing,2011)

The Ocean Between Us
Rhonda H. Bishop and Cass Barch
(AuthorHouse, 2008)

100 Days and 99 Nights
Alan Madison
(Little, Brown Young Readers, 2010)

**My Dad's Deployment: A Deployment
and Reunion Activity Book for Young Children**
Julie Labelle and Christina Rodriguez
(Elva Resa Publishers, 2009)

RESOURCES FOR ADULTS

Most installations offer service men and women
a wide variety of educational material designed
to help children cope with deployments.

In addition:

Sesame Workshop: Talk, Listen, Connect
An education outreach programme from the
makers of Sesame Street with a variety of resources
for military parents and children.
http://archive.sesameworkshop.org/tlc/

Military Families Near and Far
Also part of the Sesame Street group, this provides
web resources to help children keep in touch
with their military parents.
http://www.familiesnearandfar.org

Army Families Federation
UK based group provides advice, support for all UK
service personnel, including tips on talking to children
about deployment.
http://www.aff.org.uk/

Military Child Education Coalition
US support group that has a downloadable
document designed to help parents explain deployment
to their children.
http://www.militarychild.org/